The Hidden Heart Series
"Bullying"

Copyright © 2014 by Cindy Dahl
All rights reserved
www.cindydahl2007.wordpress.com

Art by Shaun Crum

ISBN-13: 978-1-941030-09-7

BULLYING

By Cindy Dahl

Illustrated By Shaun Crum

Hi, I am a GLíCK. You say it like /glēk/. It stands for Giving, Loving, Inspiring, Caring and Kind. I hope you enjoy my story about Sadie the cow, and how she got through a sad bullying problem.

I have hidden a heart in one of the pages; see if you can find the love in this book.

Hint: The hidden heart is in the stars.

This is a story
About Sadie the cow.
Sadie was bullied
And I'll tell you how.

Her spots are big
And her nose is wide,
But wanting friends
She couldn't hide.

But she always fell short
Of trying to fit in.
She really wanted friends,
But, where to begin?

Sadie was sad
And alone all the time.
When asked how she was
She would always say, "fine".

How she truly felt
She didn't want to say.
It hurt her heart
Day after day.

Other cows teased her
And told her "go away."
They pushed and shoved her
And didn't let her play.

One day some cows
Circled around Sadie.
They laughed and kicked her
And called her a baby.

Sadie cried and hobbled
All the way home.
She couldn't just stay
In the field and roam.

When she got home
She told her Mom and Dad
All that had happened
And just how bad.

Her parents were shocked
And didn't really know
All that Sadie went through
Wherever she'd go.

Sadie's parents told her
The reason they are mean
Is because they usually
Have low self esteem.

Sadie couldn't believe
That this could be true.
It really wasn't her fault?
She never had a clue.

The very next day
The bullies called her names,
Sadie looked and smiled,
And went on with her games.

The cows had never seen
Her stand up to mean guys.
But Sadie had done it
And looked right in their eyes.

When another cow noticed
How Sadie just smiled,
She thought it was great.
It was different and wild!

She walked over to Sadie
And said, "My name is Molly.
I liked how you did that."
She was so happy and jolly.

This made Sadie proud
And feel happy, a lot.
She wasn't for so long
She thought she forgot.

But after playing all day
With her new friend,
Sadie was so happy
She didn't want it to end.

From that moment on
They were best friends forever.
They played every day
And were always together.

Now when those bullies
Tried to mess with Sadie,
She simply smiled
And acted like a lady.

The bullies got bored
And left her alone altogether.
Now Sadie was happy
And had the best friend ever!

"No one can make you feel inferior without your consent."

– Eleanor Roosevelt

Cindy Dahl is the author of several feel good children's books including the entire "hidden heart series" where kids get to find the hidden heart in each book. "It's like finding the love in the pages of a book." Cindy's main goal with writing her books is to inspire and bring a positive message for kids at a very young age. "It is never too young to learn to be kind to one another, to feel good about yourself, and to share with others."

Cindy grew up on a farm in Northern California and currently resides in Colorado. Cindy has three grown children. She read to them often when they were young and loved watching their faces when they felt the story come alive. In her spare time, Cindy enjoys being in the great Colorado outdoors.

www.ingramcontent.com/pod-product-compliance
Lightning Source LLC
Chambersburg PA
CBHW060500240426
43661CB00006B/868